DRUG ADDICTION AND RECOVERY

Intervention and Recovery

DRUG ADDICTION AND RECOVERY

Intervention and Recovery

Michael Centore

SERIES CONSULTANT
SARA BECKER, Ph.D.
Brown University School of Public Health
Warren Alpert Medical School

MASON CREST

Mason Crest
450 Parkway Drive, Suite D
Broomall, PA 19008
www.masoncrest.com

MTM Publishing, Inc.
www.mtmpublishing.com

President: Valerie Tomaselli
Vice President, Book Development: Hilary Poole
Designer: Annemarie Redmond
Copyeditor: Peter Jaskowiak
Editorial Assistant: Andrea St. Aubin

Series ISBN: 978-1-4222-3598-0
Hardback ISBN: 978-1-4222-3605-5
E-Book ISBN: 978-1-4222-8249-6

Library of Congress Cataloging-in-Publication Data
Names: Centore, Michael, 1980- author.
Title: Intervention and recovery / by Michael Centore.
Description: Broomall, PA : Mason Crest, [2017] | Series: Drug addiction and
   recovery | Includes index.
Identifiers: LCCN 2016003952| ISBN 9781422236055 (hardback) | ISBN
   9781422235980 (series) | ISBN 9781422282496 (ebook)
Subjects: LCSH: Substance abuse—Treatment—Juvenile literature. | Drug addicts—
   Rehabilitation—Juvenile literature. | Alcoholics—Rehabilitation—Juvenile
   literature. | Drug abuse—Juvenile literature.
Classification: LCC RC564.3 .C465 2017 | DDC 362.29—dc23
LC record available at http://lccn.loc.gov/2016003952

Printed and bound in the United States of America.

First printing
9 8 7 6 5 4 3 2 1

TABLE OF CONTENTS

Key Icons to Look for:

 Words to Understand: These words with their easy-to-understand definitions will increase the reader's understanding of the text, while building vocabulary skills.

 Sidebars: This boxed material within the main text allows readers to build knowledge, gain insights, explore possibilities, and broaden their perspectives by weaving together additional information to provide realistic and holistic perspectives.

 Research Projects: Readers are pointed toward areas of further inquiry connected to each chapter. Suggestions are provided for projects that encourage deeper research and analysis.

 Text-Dependent Questions: These questions send the reader back to the text for more careful attention to the evidence presented there.

 Educational Videos: Readers can view videos by scanning our QR codes, providing them with additional educational content to supplement the text. Examples include news coverage, moments in history, speeches, iconic sports moments and much more!

 Series Glossary of Key Terms: This back-of-the-book glossary contains terminology used throughout the series. Words found here increase the reader's ability to read and comprehend higher-level books and articles in this field.

SERIES INTRODUCTION

Many adolescents in the United States will experiment with alcohol or other drugs by time they finish high school. According to a 2014 study funded by the National Institute on Drug Abuse, about 27 percent of 8th graders have tried alcohol, 20 percent have tried drugs, and 13 percent have tried cigarettes. By 12th grade, these rates more than double: 66 percent of 12th graders have tried alcohol, 50 percent have tried drugs, and 35 percent have tried cigarettes.

Adolescents who use substances experience an increased risk of a wide range of negative consequences, including physical injury, family conflict, school truancy, legal problems, and sexually transmitted diseases. Higher rates of substance use are also associated with the leading causes of death in this age group: accidents, suicide, and violent crime. Relative to adults, adolescents who experiment with alcohol or other drugs progress more quickly to a full-blown substance use disorder and have more co-occurring mental health problems.

The National Survey on Drug Use and Health (NSDUH) estimated that in 2015 about 1.3 million adolescents between the ages of 12 and 17 (5 percent of adolescents in the United States) met the medical criteria for a substance use disorder. Unfortunately, the vast majority of these

IF YOU NEED HELP NOW . . .

SAMHSA's National Helpline provides referrals for mental-health or substance-use counseling.
1-800-662-HELP (4357) or https://findtreatment.samhsa.gov

SAMHSA's National Suicide Prevention Lifeline provides crisis counseling by phone or online, 24-hours-a-day and 7 days a week.
1-800-273-TALK (8255) or http://www.suicidepreventionlifeline.org

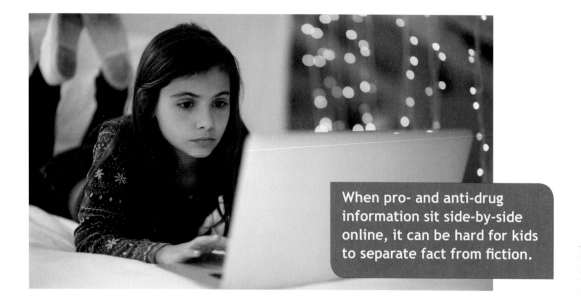

When pro- and anti-drug information sit side-by-side online, it can be hard for kids to separate fact from fiction.

adolescents did not receive treatment. Less than 10 percent of those with a diagnosis received specialty care, leaving 1.2 million adolescents with an unmet need for treatment.

The NSDUH asked the 1.2 million adolescents with untreated substance use disorders why they didn't receive specialty care. Over 95 percent said that they didn't think they needed it. The other 5 percent reported challenges finding quality treatment that was covered by their insurance. Very few treatment providers and agencies offer substance use treatment designed to meet the specific needs of adolescents. Meanwhile, numerous insurance plans have "opted out" of providing coverage for addiction treatment, while others have placed restrictions on what is covered.

Stigma about substance use is another serious problem. We don't call a person with an eating disorder a "food abuser," but we use terms like "drug abuser" to describe individuals with substance use disorders. Even treatment providers often unintentionally use judgmental words, such as describing urine screen results as either "clean" or "dirty." Underlying this language is the idea that a substance use disorder is some kind of moral failing or character flaw, and that people with these disorders deserve blame or punishment for their struggles.

And punish we do. A 2010 report by CASA Columbia found that in the United States, 65 percent of the 2.3 million people in prisons and jails met medical criteria for a substance use disorder, while another 20 percent had histories of substance use disorders, committed their crimes while under the influence of alcohol or drugs, or committed a substance-related crime. Many of these inmates spend decades in prison, but only 11 percent of them receive any treatment during their incarceration. Our society invests significantly more money in punishing individuals with substance use disorders than we do in treating them.

At a basic level, the ways our society approaches drugs and alcohol—declaring a "war on drugs," for example, or telling kids to "Just Say No!"—reflect a misunderstanding about the nature of addiction. The reality is that addiction is a disease that affects all types of people—parents and children, rich and poor, young and old. Substance use disorders stem from a complex interplay of genes, biology, and the environment, much like most physical and mental illnesses.

The way we talk about recovery, using phrases like "kick the habit" or "breaking free," also misses the mark. Substance use disorders are chronic, insidious, and debilitating illnesses. Fortunately, there are a number of effective treatments for substance use disorders. For many patients, however, the road is long and hard. Individuals recovering from substance use disorders can experience horrible withdrawal symptoms, and many will continue to struggle with cravings for alcohol or drugs. It can be a daily struggle to cope with these cravings and stay abstinent. A popular saying at Alcoholics Anonymous (AA) meetings is "one day at a time," because every day of recovery should be respected and celebrated.

There are a lot of incorrect stereotypes about individuals with substance use disorders, and there is a lot of false information about the substances, too. If you do an Internet search on the term "marijuana," for instance, two top hits are a web page by the National Institute on Drug Abuse and a page operated by Weedmaps, a medical and recreational marijuana dispensary. One of these pages publishes scientific information and one publishes pro-marijuana articles. Both pages have a high-quality, professional appearance. If you had never heard of either organization, it would be hard to know which to trust. It can be really difficult for the average person, much less the average teenager, to navigate these waters.

The topics covered in this series were specifically selected to be relevant to teenagers. About half of the volumes cover the types of drugs that they are most likely to hear about or to come in contact with. The other half cover important issues related to alcohol and other drug use (which we refer to as "drug use" in the titles for simplicity). These books cover topics such as the causes of drug use, the influence of drug use on the family, drug use and the legal system, drug use and mental health, and treatment options. Many teens will either have personal experience with these issues or will know someone who does.

This series was written to help young people get the facts about common drugs, substance use disorders, substance-related problems, and recovery. Accurate information can help adolescents to make better decisions. Students who are educated can help each other to better understand the risks and consequences of drug use. Facts also go a long way to reducing the stigma associated with substance use. We tend to fear or avoid things that we don't understand. Knowing the facts can make it easier to support each other. For students who know someone struggling with a substance use disorder, these books can also help them know what to expect. If they are worried about someone, or even about themselves, these books can help to provide some answers and a place to start.

—Sara J. Becker, Ph.D., Assistant Professor (Research), Center for Alcohol and Addictions Studies, Brown University School of Public Health, Assistant Professor (Research), Department of Psychiatry and Human Behavior, Brown University Medical School

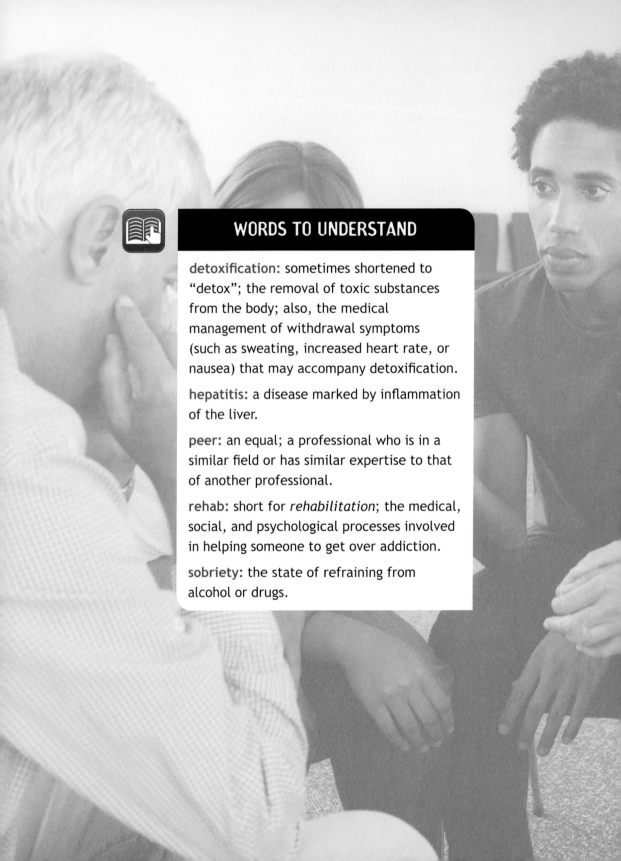

WORDS TO UNDERSTAND

detoxification: sometimes shortened to "detox"; the removal of toxic substances from the body; also, the medical management of withdrawal symptoms (such as sweating, increased heart rate, or nausea) that may accompany detoxification.

hepatitis: a disease marked by inflammation of the liver.

peer: an equal; a professional who is in a similar field or has similar expertise to that of another professional.

rehab: short for *rehabilitation*; the medical, social, and psychological processes involved in helping someone to get over addiction.

sobriety: the state of refraining from alcohol or drugs.

CHAPTER ONE

WHAT IS ADDICTION MEDICINE?

Drug and alcohol rehabilitation—or "rehab" for short—gets a lot of media attention. Television talk shows and tabloid magazines always seem to be running a new story on a celebrity who has just checked into rehab. Some reality shows feature people undergoing treatment live on camera, allowing the audience a sneak peak into a very private struggle. What used to be a sensitive, secretive topic has become a part of popular culture.

This isn't a bad thing. There's a much greater awareness of the negative consequences of addiction. Plus, stories about rehab can be inspirational. Watching someone overcome a personal obstacle to lead a happier, healthier, more fulfilling life is a reminder of our ability to grow and change. It shows us that no matter how bad a situation might seem, there is a way forward if we are willing to take that first step.

Despite this, the popularity of rehab stories in the media has led to many myths and misinformation. On television, images of plush rehab centers often glamorize treatment, making it seem more like a vacation than a form of medical care. Scenes of group-based therapies, where counselors, friends, and fellow patients gather together, can be made to look overly dramatic, like people are more interested in fighting with each other than creating a community of care and support.

But rehab is much more complex than what we see in the media. It's not just one person trying to "conquer" his or her addiction through sheer force of will, but a collaborative effort by many different people using many different treatment procedures. It can be an inspiring journey toward sobriety and a new life, but it can also be the beginning of a long and drawn-out struggle to stay clean.

The media contributes to a myth that "rehab" is a glamorous experience that's mainly for celebrities. But the reality is quite different.

MYTHS AND MISPERCEPTIONS

Movies and celebrity rehab stories have created a lot of false perceptions about addiction treatment. One is that people's lives must be a total mess before entering rehab. In reality, people can and do seek help at all stages of addiction. Another myth is that rehab is a guaranteed cure for addiction, as if just checking into a facility is a sure sign that someone is on the road to recovery. In fact, rehab never really "ends," the cravings that lead people to addiction never go away, and recovering addicts must work every day to avoid a relapse.

MEDICINE AND TREATMENT SYSTEMS

Rehab is a small part of what is known as the *addiction medicine system*. Addiction medicine is a medical specialty that deals with addictions to alcohol, drugs, tobacco, or negative habits like gambling or using the Internet too much. What's unique about addiction medicine is that professionals from all kinds of backgrounds are involved, from physicians and psychiatrists to social workers and counselors.

The ways that all these different specialists collaborate to help people who struggle with addiction form what is called an *addiction treatment system*. Treatment systems cover a large range of treatment options—from a basic, one-on-one therapy session between a patient and a counselor to a full-blown **detoxification** process where medication is needed. Treatment systems extend beyond just the patient's addiction. They may include services to help him or her find housing or a job, square away financial affairs, treat mental health disorders like depression or anxiety, or address physical health diseases that can accompany drug use, such as HIV-AIDS or **hepatitis**.

The Benchmark Recovery Center in Austin, Texas.

EVOLUTION OF ADDICTION TREATMENT

The earliest addiction medicine systems were not so much "treatments" as punishments—harsh methods of deterring people from indulging in alcohol. The ancient Egyptians, for instance, would whip people who were suspected of drunkenness, while the Turks poured molten lead down the user's throat. The Greeks had a more mystical approach, believing that the presence of amethysts while drinking would protect against drunkenness.

Addiction treatment systems have their own history in America. In the 18th century, elders from Native American tribes would counsel those struggling with addiction. These "sobriety circles" were the earliest known form of addiction treatment. In 1784, Dr. Benjamin Rush, a signer of the Declaration of Independence, wrote about the effects of alcohol on the mind and body. He was one of the first physicians to think about alcoholism as a disease, and he suggested the idea of a "sober house" where alcoholics could receive treatment. Versions of these "sober houses" sprung up across America throughout the 19th century.

The dangers of alcoholism have preoccupied us for a long time, as seen in this 1811 etching by Thomas Rowlandson.

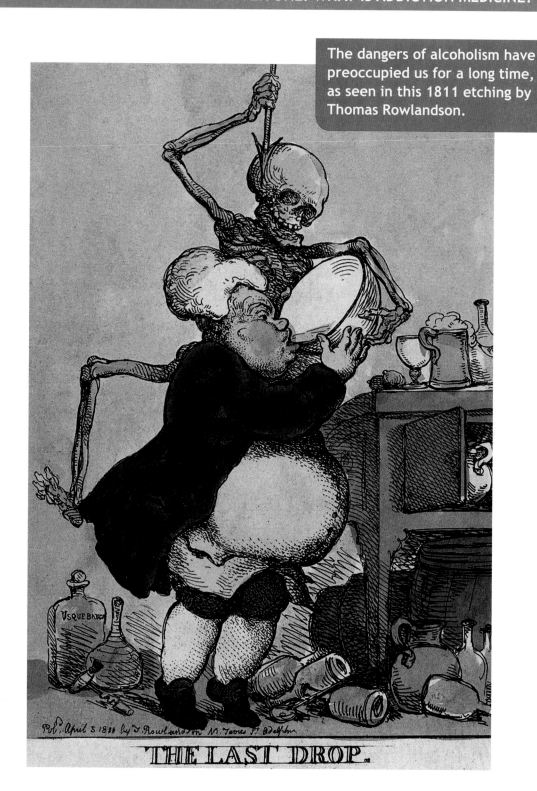

THE LAST DROP.

THE KEELEY INSTITUTE

In 1879, the first of many Keeley Institutes opened in Dwight, Illinois. This was the earliest commercial treatment center for alcoholism, meaning that people paid to stay there. It eventually expanded to more than 200 locations throughout the United States and Europe.

As modern ideas about addiction have evolved, addiction treatment systems have evolved, too. Today it is recognized that addiction is a disease rather than a personal flaw or weakness. This means that contemporary treatments are less judgmental and tailored to the needs of individual patients. They include new methods like behavioral therapy, which is a way of helping the patient identify the causes for his or her substance use and beginning to change them. Instead of focusing just on the addiction, these modern methods try to treat the whole person.

ALCOHOLICS ANONYMOUS

One of the major developments in US addiction treatment was the founding of Alcoholics Anonymous, or AA, in Akron, Ohio, in 1935. The New Yorker Bill Wilson and Akron resident Dr. Bob Smith were alcoholics who were involved with the Oxford Group, a spiritual fellowship that helped people lead well-structured lives. Wilson had been able to beat his alcoholism through his contact with the group, while Smith still struggled. During a business trip to Akron, Wilson met Smith and impressed him with his committed sobriety. Wilson shared the key to his success, which was understanding that alcoholism was a disease that could be overcome with mindfulness and commitment. With the two men working together, Smith made rapid progress. He had his last drink on June 10, 1935, which to this day is kept as the anniversary of AA.

Smith and Wilson rapidly set to work helping others in Akron and New York. After four years they reported that 100 patients had been cured. In collaboration with some of these patients, the two men wrote a book called *Alcoholics Anonymous* that outlined their system of recovery. At the center was a program known as the "12 steps" (see sidebar) that encourages members to admit their addiction, forgive themselves, and accept that sobriety was a battle to be fought day by day. Recovering alcoholics work with those who are still struggling—mirroring the original partnership between Smith and Wilson.

After *Alcoholics Anonymous* was published in 1939, the group grew quickly. By 1950 there were over 100,000 people in recovery worldwide thanks to AA. As of 2015, AA has over 2 million members around the globe.

The house in Akron, Ohio, where Dr. Robert Smith lived when he and Bill Wilson developed Alcoholics Anonymous. The house was declared a National Historic Landmark in 2012.

A key part of AA's approach involves pairing up a person who is farther along in his or her sobriety, and who can help guide and advise someone else who might be struggling.

Its widespread influence has spawned related groups for other types of addictions, including Narcotics Anonymous, Overeaters Anonymous, and Workaholics Anonymous, and its methodology has greatly informed the ways that many substance use counselors practice today.

While the 12-step method has worked for thousands of people, it still has its critics. Some medical professionals say that there isn't enough data to accurately gauge the method's effectiveness; that it was developed at an earlier time, when knowledge of addiction and the brain was not what it is today; and that it only offers total abstinence and self-surrender as a way of overcoming addiction, when in fact there are other ways of treating unhealthy habits. A medicine such as naltrexone is just one example.

Another common criticism is that the 12-step method places too much emphasis on notions of a "higher power." Both medical professionals and

THE 12 STEPS

The famous "12 steps" of Alcoholics Anonymous have served as guidelines for many people trying to overcome addiction. They help the user reclaim control of his or her life through right mindfulness, community support, and total self-honesty. In their traditional order, they are:

1. We admitted we were powerless over alcohol—that our lives had become unmanageable.
2. Came to believe that a Power greater than ourselves could restore us to sanity.
3. Made a decision to turn our will and our lives over to the care of God *as we understood Him.*
4. Made a searching and fearless moral inventory of ourselves.
5. Admitted to God, to ourselves, and to another human being the exact nature of our wrongs.
6. Were entirely ready to have God remove all these defects of character.
7. Humbly asked Him to remove our shortcomings.
8. Made a list of all persons we had harmed, and became willing to make amends to them all.
9. Made direct amends to such people wherever possible, except when to do so would injure them or others.
10. Continued to take personal inventory, and when we were wrong, promptly admitted it.
11. Sought through prayer and meditation to improve our conscious contact with God *as we understood Him,* praying only for knowledge of His will for us and the power to carry that out.
12. Having had a spiritual awakening as the result of these steps, we tried to carry this message to alcoholics, and to practice these principles in all our affairs.

those struggling with use disorders can be put off by this overtly religious language, especially if they are not people of faith. In response, some secular support groups have embraced the 12 steps but shifted the focus from a religious power to the power of the individual, friends, and family.

OTHER HEALTH SYSTEMS

In addition to addiction treatment, there are two other major healthcare systems—mental and physical. Mental health systems include psychiatrists, therapists, and other professionals who work with patients with conditions such as depression, anxiety, and other disorders. Physical health systems treat ailments of the body, like sicknesses or diseases.

While both the mental and physical treatment systems may help people suffering from addiction, this is not necessarily their specialty. Not all mental health patients have addictions, and while physicians may treat health problems stemming from addictions (like hepatitis), they rarely have the time or resources to treat the addiction itself.

Medical doctors focus on the impact that substance abuse has on physical health.

One thing that makes the addiction treatment system unique is that it developed on its own, apart from the mental and physical systems. Until the 1950s, use disorders were rarely discussed in public, because they were seen as an embarrassment rather than illnesses to be cured. It was hard to find doctors who had the knowledge or were even willing to treat them. People who were interested in helping others with addictions had to seek each other out. Many were recovering addicts themselves. They traded ideas, information, and different methods of treatment. Unlike the mental and physical systems, they were open to methods that didn't come from the scientific community, like AA's Twelve Step program. This willingness to "think outside the box" and their strong reliance on **peer** support led to the development of modern addiction medicine.

TEXT-DEPENDENT QUESTIONS

1. What are some major ways that addiction treatment systems have evolved since the 18th century?
2. How are addiction treatment systems different from the other health-care treatment systems?
3. What are some of the benefits of the 12 steps? What are some of the criticisms?

RESEARCH PROJECT

Research a professional position within the field of addiction treatment systems, such as an addiction physician, a psychologist, a counselor, or a social worker. Write a brief report summarizing what this person does, the type of training involved, and how he or she contributes to an addiction treatment team.

WORDS TO UNDERSTAND

illicit: something that is not permitted or is against the law.

intervention: (1) when family, friends, and others gather around a person with a use disorder and urge him or her to seek treatment; (2) in the field of addiction medicine, generally used to mean any form of treatment.

recovery: the process an individual undergoes to move from substance use disorder to sobriety, which may include the medical, social, and psychological treatments of rehab.

relapse: when someone who is in recovery from substance use disorder begins to use substances again.

CHAPTER TWO

THE RECOVERY PROCESS

People enter the addiction medicine system through many different routes. Those who get into trouble with the law because of their addictions—perhaps by buying illicit drugs or stealing to pay for them, or driving while drunk multiple times—might be sent to treatment by a judge. Others may go at the request of their families or friends, as in the case of an intervention. Still others might be made physically unwell because of substances, causing them to enter a form of medical treatment. Occasionally, people will recognize that they have a problem and seek treatment on their own. Whatever road takes them there, the journey through the treatment process can be a physically and emotionally intense experience. Fortunately, most addiction medicine programs have methods in place to make sure patients stay on track.

Sometimes an interaction with the justice system forces the issue of a need for drug or alcohol treatment.

RECOVERY AND THE STAGES OF CHANGE

Recovery and rehabilitation are similar words, but they have slightly different meanings in the field of addiction medicine. Recovery is the overall process of kicking an addiction—a process of growth and development through which individuals get their health back, take ownership of their decisions, and create a life without dependence on substances. A stint in a rehab facility is often a part of recovery, but recovery continues even once someone is out of rehab. This is because the craving to use the substance may never go away with a use disorder. Since avoiding a relapse is a lifelong commitment that doesn't just magically end, people who have completed rehab prefer to say they are "in recovery" rather than "recovered."

Patients who have gone through rehab often must stay on top of their urges, working daily to fulfill themselves with healthier habits. "Urge surfing" is a technique used in recovery programs. It acknowledges that cravings for drugs and alcohol can be very strong. Rather than try to shut them out, patients are taught to "surf" their urge until it passes, riding it like a surfer does a wave.

There are different ideas about when recovery actually begins. Some professionals say it's when a person quits using alcohol or drugs. Others see it as a process that starts the moment someone realizes he or she has a problem. Almost 30 years ago, two well-known alcohol researchers, Drs. James O. Prochaska and Carlo C. DiClemente, developed a model of change to help professionals understand their patients with addiction problems and motivate them to change. Their model was based on observations of the common phases people move through when changing problem behaviors. Today, the six stages of change are often used by patients and treatment specialists to talk about the recovery process. The stages are:

1. **Precontemplation.** At this stage, the person denies that he or she has a problem. The person is unwilling to change, believing that the positives of substance use (like having fun with their friends) outweigh the negatives (like feeling depressed the following day).

2. **Contemplation.** At this stage, the person becomes conscious of his or her problem. The person begins to see that the negatives of their addiction outweigh the positives and explore the options for treatment. Still, the person makes no commitment to change.

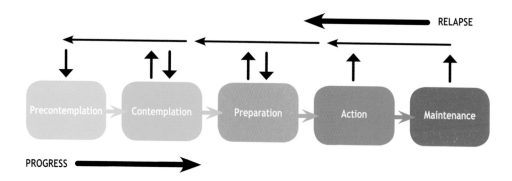

The states of change. Note the arrows, which suggest that the path to sobriety is not always a straight line.

When a person begins to realize that the bad parts of his or her drug or alcohol use are outweighing the good parts, that's called the contemplation stage.

3. **Preparation.** This is the moment when someone decides to make a change. The person starts to make a plan for how to beat addiction. The person may begin looking into treatment facilities.

4. **Action.** This stage is when someone takes definitive steps toward change. The individual might enter a rehab facility, find a counselor, or start going to AA meetings.

5. **Maintenance.** A person at this stage has started to live a life away from alcohol or drugs. Getting to this phase usually takes at least three to six months after the action phase. It becomes easier to stay away from substances, though the danger of a relapse is always there. If a person relapses, it isn't the end of the world; he or she can learn from the mistake and recommit to an earlier stage of change.

6. **Termination.** The final stage of recovery, when a person feels fully capable of living without substances. He or she has good health, a place

to live, a sense of purpose, and a supportive community. He or she is also capable of dealing with the minor disruptions of life (like stress at work) that used to trigger the urge to drink or do drugs.

TREATMENT WITHIN THE STAGES OF CHANGE

For therapists and other addiction specialists, the stages of change model helps determine the best way to treat patients at a given time. Those in the precontemplation or contemplation stage may not want to change their behavior right away. They may have entered therapy because someone else told them to, like a family member or a school counselor, rather than because they wanted to themselves. The lure of alcohol or drugs can be incredibly strong. It isn't always easy for people with addictions to see just how negative their effects can be.

RESENTMENT AND EUPHORIA

"Dry drunk syndrome" can get in the way of an alcoholic's full recovery. This is when a person has stopped drinking but is not willing to replace alcohol with healthier lifestyle habits. Rather than try to create a new, happier life, the person focuses on feeling deprived of alcohol. He or she may become resentful at family, friends, and counselors. The mean-spiritedness of dry drunk syndrome can be as rough on other people as the person's behavior when he or she was drinking.

On the opposite end of the spectrum, "pink cloud syndrome" is when someone feels so good about recovery that they think they are invincible. Living in a "pink cloud" of fantasy and optimism, the person no longer puts the necessary work into staying sober. If the person is not careful, this unrealistic positivity can lead to a relapse.

RECOVERY COMMUNITY ORGANIZATIONS

Recovery community organizations (RCOs) are a huge part of the addiction medicine system. These are grassroots organizations that foster dialogue between people in recovery, addiction treatment specialists, governmental and legal organizations, and the health and medical fields. A group called Faces and Voices of Recovery (facesandvoicesofrecovery.org) unites many of these RCOs to maximize their influence and leadership potential.

The month of September is an important one for many RCOs, as this is when the Substance Abuse and Mental Health Services Administration (SAMHSA) sponsors an annual "National Recovery Month" to celebrate those in recovery and educate the public about substance use disorders.

In the early stages of change, therapists simply want patients to think about their relationship to substances. Is it a healthy one? Does it cause depression or have other negative effects? The goal is to motivate the patient to want to change. A key assumption here is that a patient will not change unless she or he really wants to. One treatment approach that is often used at this stage is called motivational interviewing (MI). In MI,

In motivational interviewing, the therapist tries to help the client come to a personal decision to change behavior, rather than forcing that change on the person.

the therapist doesn't just tell a patient to change, but instead leads the patient to make the decision for him or herself. For instance, instead of telling the patient he or she has got to give up alcohol "or else," the therapist will listen to the reasons why the patient likes to drink. Together, they will discuss whether these reasons outweigh the negative effects. The patient's intelligence and free will are respected throughout the process. The philosophy behind this approach is that if the decision to change comes from the patient and not the therapist, it is much stronger.

Once the patient admits he or she might have a problem, the therapist can begin providing more detailed and action-oriented treatment plans. By the action and maintenance stages, the therapist is working with the patient to turn these plans into reality. This involves helping the patient learn to deal with temptation, create new lifestyle habits that aren't based on drugs or alcohol, and develop strategies to prevent a relapse.

TEXT-DEPENDENT QUESTIONS

1. How is recovery different from rehab?
2. What are the six stages of change, and what are the signs of each?
3. What is the overall strategy of motivational interviewing, and how is it accomplished?

RESEARCH PROJECT

Find a recovery community organization in your area. Research the organization (perhaps by interviewing a member or one of its leaders) to find out what the organization does, what types of events it holds, and how people can get involved. Write a brief report summarizing your findings. You might start by looking at the Faces and Voices of Recovery website (http://www.facesandvoicesofrecovery.org/who/regions), which has gathered information about resources in different parts of the country.

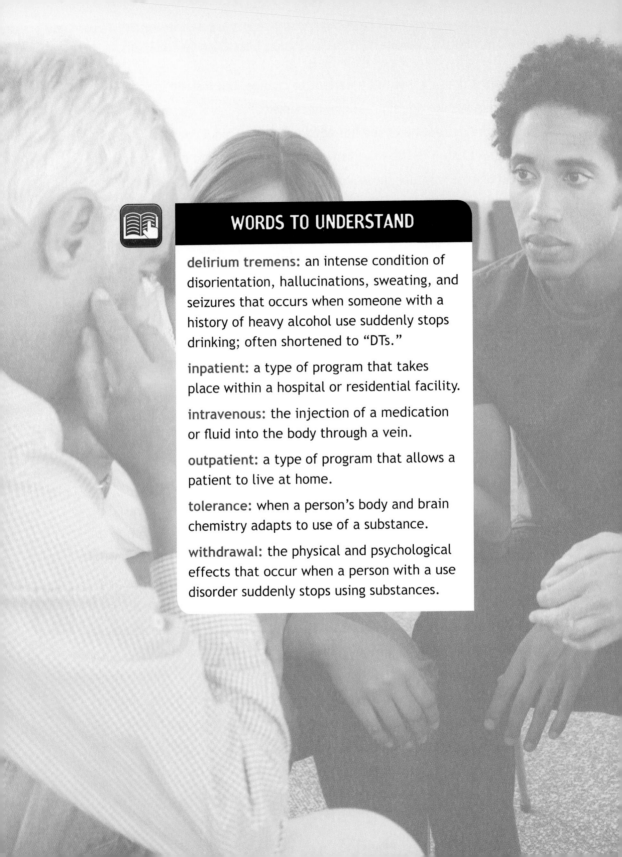

WORDS TO UNDERSTAND

delirium tremens: an intense condition of disorientation, hallucinations, sweating, and seizures that occurs when someone with a history of heavy alcohol use suddenly stops drinking; often shortened to "DTs."

inpatient: a type of program that takes place within a hospital or residential facility.

intravenous: the injection of a medication or fluid into the body through a vein.

outpatient: a type of program that allows a patient to live at home.

tolerance: when a person's body and brain chemistry adapts to use of a substance.

withdrawal: the physical and psychological effects that occur when a person with a use disorder suddenly stops using substances.

CHAPTER THREE

FIRST STEPS TOWARD SOBRIETY

One of the traps of drugs and alcohol is that they can hurt a person's ability to see that he or she even has a problem. The longer someone depends on substances, the more the substances can become the central focus of the person's life. Users get caught up in their own little worlds, oblivious to how their behavior is affecting their health and their relationships with others. In these cases, something needs to happen for the person to be willing to enter treatment—such as getting in trouble at work or school, or getting in trouble with the law. One way to try and get someone to recognize his or her substance use problems and agree to enter treatment is through an intervention.

INTERVENTION

An intervention is when family and friends confront the user and urge him or her to seek treatment. Interventions have turned up in the plotlines of countless popular television shows, including *Real Housewives of Beverly Hills*, *The Real World*, *Celebrity Apprentice*, *Dr. Phil*, and, appropriately, *Intervention*.

The key to a successful intervention is not to make accusing, degrading, or humiliating comments that give the conversation a negative tone. Instead, family and friends are encouraged to share their concerns about the person's substance use in an open and caring manner. They need to communicate that they want the best for the person. This means suggesting options for treatment, and allowing the person to choose which ones might be best. It also means giving a firm but fair account of what each member of the intervention team will do if the person does *not* choose to accept treatment. For example, a friend who has been emotionally hurt by the user might say that he or she will have no choice but to cut off the friendship if the person doesn't get help.

Interventions can be as tough not only for the subject of the intervention, but also for everybody else involved in it. Friends and family members undoubtedly have negative emotions of their own that are totally natural and understandable. As the intervention must be a space of healing and dialogue, rather than judgment and negativity, a main aim of the intervention leader is to balance the delicate feelings of the participants. This is why it is good to have a professional, impartial substance-abuse counselor to coordinate the intervention team.

A counselor has knowledge of the various treatment options and can prepare everyone for the different ways the person might react. Being the subject of an intervention is upsetting, and resistance and hostility are common responses. When it comes time for the intervention itself, the counselor will lead the discussion, keeping everyone calm and focused. After the intervention, if the person agrees to change, the counselor will help get him or her into a treatment program as soon as possible. Delays allow the person to reconsider the decision or go on one last "bender" before committing to treatment.

An experienced counselor can help keep the discussion on track.

With all the talk of interventions in pop culture, people can begin to think that they are the necessary way for someone to start treatment. In fact, they are one of several paths toward an initial decision to start treatment.

DETOXIFICATION

When a person is addicted to drugs or alcohol, his or her system adapts to the substance. This is called **tolerance**. The substance changes the person's brain chemistry, and he or she needs to use it just to feel normal. If the person suddenly stops using, the body tries to rebalance itself. This rapid shift can lead to all sorts of physical and psychological complications, which are known as **withdrawal symptoms**. These can include heavy sweating, seizures, insomnia, and vomiting. The detoxification process both cleanses the person of the substance and fights withdrawal symptoms.

Not everybody's withdrawal symptoms are equally strong. Because of this, there are different levels of detoxification available in the addiction

STEPS TO A SUCCESSFUL INTERVENTION

Interventions can be tough to organize. A person's family and friends may have conflicting ideas about the best way to help, and finally speaking about the issue face-to-face can be difficult. The Mayo Clinic, a well-known medical research group, lists the seven steps of a successful intervention:

1. After deciding to hold an intervention, contact a professional and begin to plan. Find other family and friends willing to help.
2. Begin to research the person's addiction and the types of treatment programs available.
3. Select a few people from the group who will physically participate in the intervention. Start to practice what you will say during the intervention. Make sure you balance emotional responses to the problem with factual, pragmatic solutions.
4. Decide what you will do if the person rejects the intervention.
5. Plan in advance what you will say during the intervention.
6. Have the intervention itself. Be sure to communicate in a loving and supportive manner, but stress the need for treatment.
7. Follow up after the intervention. This is a crucial step—if the team just stays together for the intervention and does not provide continued support afterward, the person may feel neglected and relapse.

treatment system. Not all patients require a formal detox, but for those who do, the programs are an important part of the recovery process.

Outpatient detox allows a person to travel back and forth between home and a hospital or treatment facility. This is a good option for less intense symptoms. In these cases, medical staff do a routine physical to check the person's condition, look at the history of his or her substance use, and create a detox plan. This may involve prescribing drugs that help alleviate insomnia and nervousness. It may also involve giving the patient intravenous doses of vitamins and minerals that have been lost through substance misuse. Outpatient detox costs less and allows the patient greater freedom. The disadvantage is that the patient may be able to access substances while away from the detox facility, a temptation that could lead to relapse.

Inpatient detox is when the patient lives at the hospital or treatment facility for a set period of time, usually anywhere from 3 to 14 days. This way, medical staff can monitor his or her condition, adjusting care as necessary. They may have to administer drugs like methadone to help wean the patient off of heavy narcotics. Inpatient is a better choice for people with more severe withdrawal symptoms, like the combination of seizures, hallucinations, and disorientation known as **delirium tremens** that accompanies extreme cases of alcohol detox. It is more expensive than outpatient, but there's security in knowing the patient will be kept away from substances until the process is complete.

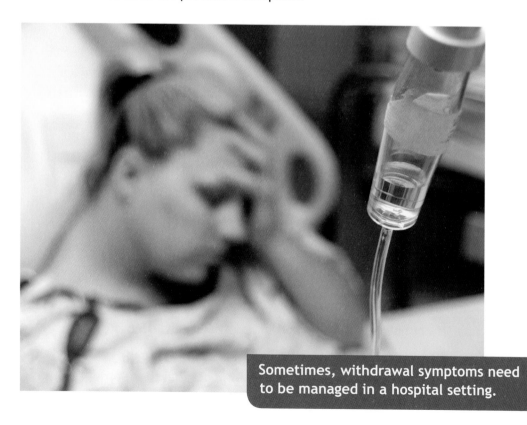

Sometimes, withdrawal symptoms need to be managed in a hospital setting.

THE DANGERS OF SELF-DETOX

For those with serious alcohol or drug addictions, trying to quit "cold turkey" without proper medical attention can be incredibly dangerous—even fatal. Suddenly stopping alcohol intake after serious, long-term alcohol addiction can cause heart seizures that may lead to death. There are medications that can help with the detox process, but the addict likely lacks the focus and clarity to keep track of the dosage. Similarly, opiate detox should never be attempted alone. The withdrawal symptoms from heroin are agonizing, and the user lacks the proper coping skills to overcome his or her cravings. He or she will likely go back to using if there is no oversight from doctors and counselors.

People who use opiates need medical attention when they quit; going "cold turkey" can be dangerous.

Whether a person needs a detox program and whether it should be inpatient or outpatient are important questions. Medical professionals evaluate a person's history of substance use, overall physical and emotional health, willingness to fight their addiction, potential for relapse, and the strength of their family's support before making a decision.

There is a process called rapid detoxification that can be completed in 4 to 8 hours—much faster than either inpatient or outpatient models. In rapid detox, the patient is placed under anesthesia and given powerful drugs that detoxify the body and fight withdrawal symptoms. It is mostly used for narcotic addictions. There are many risks, however, as the process takes a toll on the body and makes the person feel terrible for several days. In addition, anesthetics themselves can be dangerous for many people.

After a successful detox, the patient is ready for the next major step: rehabilitation and building a life without drugs and alcohol.

TEXT-DEPENDENT QUESTIONS

1. What is an intervention, and what are some methods and techniques used to make sure it is successful?
2. What is the difference between inpatient and outpatient forms of treatment?
3. Why is detoxification often the first step in an overall rehabilitation program?

RESEARCH PROJECT

Select a substance (e.g., alcohol, opiates, or cocaine) and research the withdrawal symptoms affiliated with it and the specific ways doctors treat them. Write a brief summary of your findings, including medications that may be used in treatment.

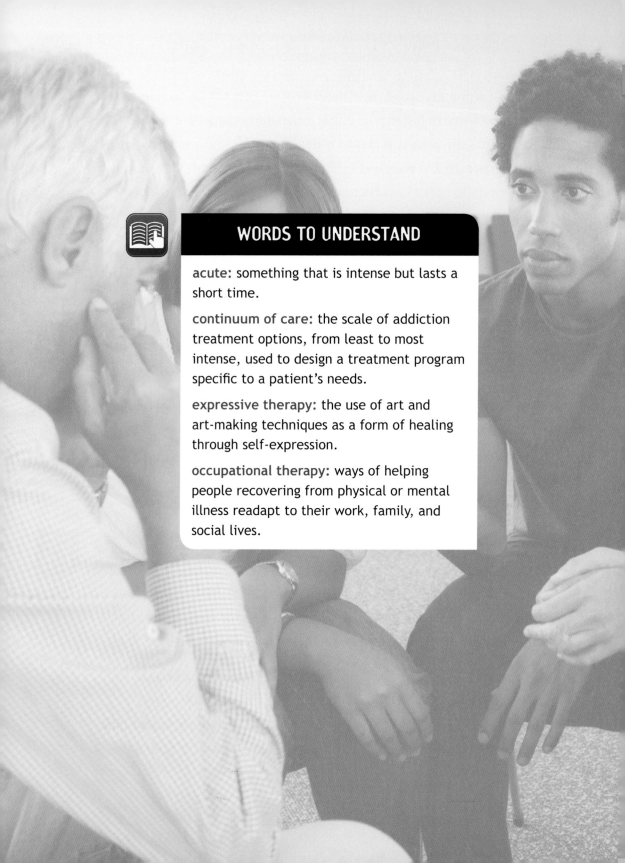

WORDS TO UNDERSTAND

acute: something that is intense but lasts a short time.

continuum of care: the scale of addiction treatment options, from least to most intense, used to design a treatment program specific to a patient's needs.

expressive therapy: the use of art and art-making techniques as a form of healing through self-expression.

occupational therapy: ways of helping people recovering from physical or mental illness readapt to their work, family, and social lives.

CHAPTER FOUR

LEVELS OF CARE

The addiction-treatment process is different for everyone. Some people need intensive rehab programs that involve round-the-clock medical care. Others don't need to check into a hospital or rehab center, but still must attend therapy groups several times a week. A few may be able to battle their addiction with only a weekly visit to a treatment counselor along with the support of family and friends. These various levels of care help people with all types of addictions find ways to live without substances.

THE CONTINUUM OF CARE

Not every addiction patient needs a complete medically supervised detox. For many patients, counseling is sufficient. As with the detoxification process, there are two main types of substance treatment programs: inpatient and outpatient. Inpatient programs keep the patient in a hospital or residence for a certain amount of time, while outpatient programs let him or her live at home.

Both inpatient and outpatient programs have different levels of intensity, based on the patient's needs. Together, these levels are known as the **continuum of care**. There are five levels in all: medically managed inpatient services, inpatient services (where patients are committed to a hospital or residence), intensive outpatient services (where patients spend some time in a hospital setting), outpatient services, and early intervention. The most serious addiction cases may need an inpatient stay, while less serious cases

Counseling is often a key part of addiction treatment.

RELAPSE TRIGGERS

A relapse can happen at any point during the stages of change, and it can occur for many different reasons. Therapists have an acronym to describe the most common triggers: HALT (for the triggers hungry, angry, lonely, and tired). Many patients and professionals have also acknowledged the importance of another relapse trigger: boredom. When someone in recovery experiences one of these emotions, they know the urge to use may not be far behind. If a person does relapse, therapists are trained to help him or her see it as an opportunity for growth rather than as a failure.

Feelings of hunger, anger, loneliness, or tiredness can all be triggers for substance use.

need either intensive outpatient or outpatient treatments, or a combination of the two. Early intervention is the strategy of identifying those with the potential for use disorders at a young age, educating them, and giving them the tools they need to beat addiction before it starts.

INPATIENT SERVICES

Residential or inpatient services are types of treatment where a patient lives in either a special residence or hospital setting for a specific amount

Group therapy can help build a sense of community, reminding people in recovery that they are not alone.

of time. Stays can be anywhere from two to 28 days or more, depending on how severe the situation is. With diverse staff supervised by a physician, patients work on relapse-prevention skills, learn concrete coping skills, and practice new lifestyle habits. Some residential treatment centers offer expressive therapies like art, music, or dance.

There are many advantages to inpatient therapy. Free from the obligations of their day-to-day lives, patients can work on getting sober without any distractions. There is also a built-in sense of community, as patients in recovery share many similar experiences. This makes for open and honest communication and a compassionate, nonjudgmental atmosphere. A set schedule helps patients avoid the boredom that can lead to substance use.

Some people may have continuing medical or psychiatric problems related to substance withdrawal. These patients may need a more intensive inpatient service known as acute care. This approach has many of the same

EXPRESS YOURSELF

The goal of expressive therapy is to get the patient in touch with his or her imagination. Through writing, drawing, or other forms of expression, the person can realize new aspects of his or her personality. This can lead to more self-knowledge and a better understanding of the roots of addiction.

features as normal inpatient treatment, but doctors must visit daily to ensure the patient's health and safety and manage any medications. Acute care usually only lasts for a short period after the detox process. If the patient makes progress, he or she is allowed to move to regular inpatient care.

There are two other long-term residential options for people in recovery: a therapeutic treatment community (TTC), and a sober living home. A TCC is primarily for people with long histories of substance misuse. Living together in a supervised home, residents share chores, activities,

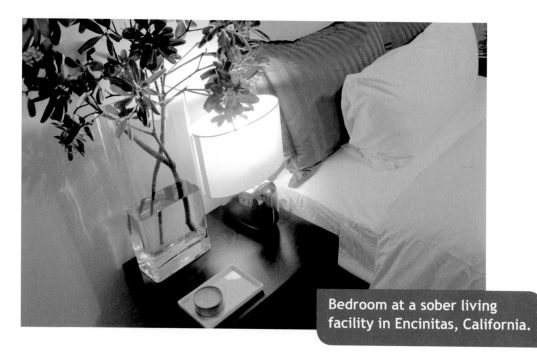

Bedroom at a sober living facility in Encinitas, California.

therapy sessions, and meals. Through this process, they help to heal each other, developing social skills and other positive lifestyle habits away from the influence of substances.

Sober living homes are similar to TCCs, but they allow residents a bit more freedom. They are sometimes called "halfway houses," because they are "halfway" between a rehab facility and regular daily life. Residents often work a job during the day, and they are expected to pay for rent, groceries, and other expenses. However, they have strictly enforced curfews and must take random drug tests to prove they are sober. This extra sense of discipline helps people in recovery commit to living a substance-free life.

OUTPATIENT SERVICES

For those with strong family support systems and a willingness to change their habits, outpatient therapies are the preferred option. These allow people to keep their jobs and live their lives as "normally" as possible while undergoing treatment. Outpatient therapy can take several different forms: individual therapy involving one therapist and one patient, family therapy involving the whole family in treatment, and group therapy involving multiple patients.

Partial hospitalization is the most intensive form of outpatient therapy. Here, patients spend full six- to eight-hour

According to the American Academy of Family Physicians, the drug diazepam (also known as Valium) can help people with mild alcohol withdrawal symptoms.

days in a hospital setting under the care of medical staff, psychiatrists, therapists, and social workers. They may receive medication for withdrawal symptoms or other psychiatric conditions. Patients may learn job skills, get educational assistance, or participate in occupational therapy. Partial hospitalization is very helpful for patients transitioning into or out of more intensive inpatient therapies.

Intensive outpatient therapy is a stepped-up level of care for those who need a little more structure than basic outpatient therapy. Therapy sessions are still the main component, but they are usually held in a special treatment facility instead of a therapist's office. There are also more sessions per week—usually three to four hours per day, three to five days per week.

Therapy can also be offered via group or family sessions. Group sessions allow patients to share stories, support each other, and learn to socialize without drugs or alcohol. Family therapy sessions help patients see how their behavior affects their loved ones. This can be a powerful motivator to change for the better.

Individual therapy sessions typically take place once or twice a week at the therapist's office or, in some cases, at the patient's school or home. The main focus is getting the recovering person to think about *why* he or she turns to drugs or alcohol. Is it boredom? Loneliness? A need to escape? The therapist helps the person address these underlying issues. The therapist and the patient work one-on-one to develop new behaviors and thought patterns to break the cycle of substance misuse.

DIFFERENT FORMS OF THERAPY

There are four main forms of therapy used in outpatient services. Some therapy programs combine these different approaches into a package of services.

- **Motivational interviewing.** In this approach (discussed in chapter two), the therapist lets a patient make his or her own decisions, guiding the process but not giving ultimatums. The therapist and the patient discuss what motivates the patient to use substances and the reasons for change.

- **Cognitive-behavioral therapy (CBT).** CBT helps patients address how they think and behave in situations that trigger substance use. Over time, the therapy introduces new ways of coping with these situations without dependence on substances.

- **Motivational incentives.** Sometimes more formally called "contingency management," motivational incentives are things like gift cards, vouchers, or prizes given to reward a patient for staying sober. Even if the monetary value of these rewards is low, studies show that they are still a powerful incentive for patients in recovery.

- **Family therapy.** This is an approach that involves the entire family in the patient's treatment. This approach is often used with adolescent patients, since adolescents often live at home and are influenced so much by their families. There are many different types of family therapy, but the key goals are to identify patterns of behavior in the family that might be contributing to the patient's use, modify family interactions to promote healthy alternatives to substance use, and improve family communication.

Family therapy helps users understand how their behavior affects the people they love.

WHEN THE CHIPS ARE DOWN

AA members receive "chips" that mark how long they have been sober: a 30-day chip, for example, or a one-year chip. These chips have no monetary value but they are highly prized

AA medallions.

by AA members because of what they represent. The chips come in different colors, each representing a time span of sobriety: a white chip represents one day of being sober, a red chip three months, and a blue chip a full year without a drink.

The tradition of the AA chip is believed to go back to 1942 in Indianapolis, when a local leader of an AA group began distributing them to members. Another possible source of origin is Sister Ignatia of Akron, Ohio, a nun who worked with recovering alcoholics. Sister Ignatia gave out religious medallions to her patients upon their release. The custom may have morphed over the years into the sobriety coin.

While not every AA group uses chips, those members who do are reported to feel a strong motivation to carry on in their journeys of sobriety. The chips serve as a reminder of how much progress they've made. Having a physical object to focus on can encourage people to think twice before relapsing. In today's digital world, there are even versions of sobriety coins that AA members can download to use as computer screensavers.

THE ED EFFECT

Acute hospitalization is a short-term form of care for a severe illness, injury, or other trauma. It is often connected to a visit to a hospital's emergency department (ED; sometimes also called ER for "emergency room"). Many acute hospitalizations and ED visits are brought about by drug and alcohol misuse. In 2011, over 5 million of the 125 million ED visits in the United States were related to drugs. This was a 100 percent increase from 2004. Of these, 1.25 million involved illegal drugs, 1.24 million involved nonmedical use of prescription drugs, and 0.61 million involved life-threatening combinations of drugs and alcohol. Substance misuse not only harms individuals, but it also puts an even greater strain on EDs that are already overcrowded.

There are millions of drug-related ED admissions every year.

EARLY INTERVENTION STRATEGIES

Early intervention strategies are an important defense against more serious substance misuse later in life. They can be used to reduce risk factors for addiction in adolescents, as well as help adults guard against the possibility of a use disorder.

One early intervention strategy that is growing in popularity is called SBIRT, which stands for Screening, Brief Intervention, and Referral to

Treatment. SBIRT is part of a normal health-care routine, like a checkup at a doctor's office. It screens all types of people and attempts to identify those prone to substance use disorders. They may be "risky drinkers" who drink more than the average recommended amount, have a history of use disorder in their family, or even be low-level drinkers who need further information about the effects of alcohol on the body. The goal of a program like SBIRT is to make sure people do not "bottom out" before adopting safe and healthy lifestyle habits.

TEXT-DEPENDENT QUESTIONS

1. What are the levels of the continuum of care, and why are they together called a "continuum"?
2. What are some therapies used in outpatient treatment?
3. Why is inpatient therapy better for people with serious addiction problems?

RESEARCH PROJECT

Research an inpatient and outpatient treatment facility in your area. Using either printed literature from each facility or information on a website, compare and contrast the approaches of the facilities. Write a brief summary of your findings, including the types of therapies used.

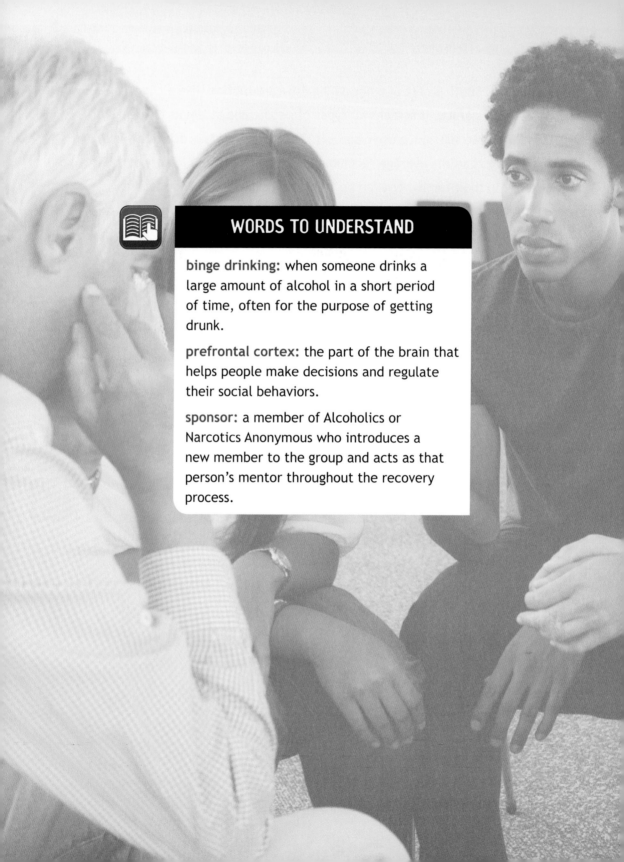

WORDS TO UNDERSTAND

binge drinking: when someone drinks a large amount of alcohol in a short period of time, often for the purpose of getting drunk.

prefrontal cortex: the part of the brain that helps people make decisions and regulate their social behaviors.

sponsor: a member of Alcoholics or Narcotics Anonymous who introduces a new member to the group and acts as that person's mentor throughout the recovery process.

CHAPTER FIVE

TEENS AND RECOVERY

People heal at various paces, and different therapies work better for different types of people. And the truth is, some have to work harder than others at maintaining sobriety. There are important differences in treatment between adolescents and adults. While there are many overlaps in methods, such as family therapy, adolescents have specific needs that must be addressed. While adults are more fully formed and have more ingrained habits, adolescents are still going through many physical and emotional changes. This adds another layer of complexity to an already difficult substance use disorder.

THE ADOLESCENT BRAIN

A main factor in adolescent addiction is that the part of the brain responsible for controlling impulses—the **prefrontal cortex**—is not finished developing until the mid-20s. This is one reason that adolescents are

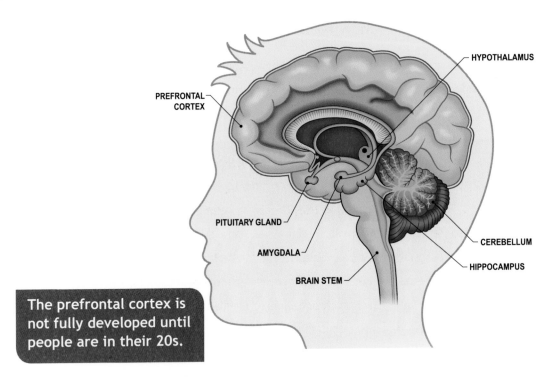

HYPOTHALAMUS

PREFRONTAL CORTEX

PITUITARY GLAND

AMYGDALA

BRAIN STEM

CEREBELLUM

HIPPOCAMPUS

The prefrontal cortex is not fully developed until people are in their 20s.

much more attracted to exciting, risky behaviors than adults. They have an urge to try new and exciting things, to establish their own sense of self apart from their families, but they may have difficulty predicting how their choices will affect their lives. They are also more susceptible to peer pressure, though that can still play a role in adult addiction.

Because adolescent brains are still developing, the effects of drugs and alcohol and the possibility for long-term misuse are heightened. Use can also lead to many other problems, like a decline in school performance or sudden withdrawal from family and friends.

There are physical factors involved, too. Recent studies have shown that teens have greater tolerance for negative effects of alcohol, such as hangovers, that may dissuade adults from drinking. This may lead to binge drinking, because teens are less aware of how much they are actually imbibing. Chronic binge drinking can cause long-term problems with brain development and memory. It also creates an unhealthy pattern of misuse that may continue into adulthood.

ADOLESCENT APPROACHES TO THERAPY

Since there are differences in the nature of their disorders, it makes sense that adults and adolescents differ in their ideas about therapy as well. For one, adolescents are far less likely to seek treatment for themselves. A big motivator for people to get help is the experience of negative consequences (like getting arrested or losing lots of money) brought about by substance use. Since teens who use substances have done so for a shorter amount of time, they probably have fewer of these experiences, and they therefore have less direct motivation to change. Also, teens are still developing the self-knowledge and self-awareness that allows them to judge their own behavior; it can be tough for them to tell whether their substance use is causing harm to themselves or to others.

Because of this, adolescents often come to treatment at someone else's request—a concerned parent, a court system, a school counselor. Teens may see this as one more in a long list of negative experiences with authority figures. They might begin treatment with distrust and resentment. This can make it hard for them to speak openly with the very people who are trying to help them. It makes approaches like motivational interviewing all the more important for adolescents.

Another key consideration for teens is family involvement. No matter how independent teens feel, they still depend on their parents or guardians for

COMMUNITY REINFORCEMENT

Because teens are highly influenced by their social lives, a behavioral therapy known as Adolescent Community Reinforcement Approach (or A-CRA) is often used with younger patients. Here, therapists work with teens and their families to replace negative influences with healthier alternatives. There are 17 different A-CRA activities, such as role playing, that help adolescents build a social life away from drugs and alcohol. In the process they find what within them will truly make them happy.

USING TO COMPETE

We often think of adolescents using drugs or alcohol to look cool or fit in with their friends. What is rarely mentioned is how students might use drugs to get an edge on others, either academically and athletically. Though these seem to be "healthy" motives, they can just as easily lead to the misuse of stimulants such as Adderall or anabolic steroids.   You might check out other volumes in this set, such as *Prescription Drugs*, *Performance-Enhancing Drugs*, and *Stimulants* for more information on those aspects of substance use.

Some students abuse prescription medication because they hope it will give them an advantage in studying.

the base necessities of food, shelter, and emotional support. Improving the lines of communication between family members is a key step in adolescent treatment and recovery. Specific family therapies can go a long way in helping. Family behavior therapy (FBT) connects use disorders to other problems in life, such as abuse, depression, or joblessness. Multidimensional family therapy (MDFT) analyzes an adolescent addict from multiple angles, including his or her relationship to family, friends, and community. MDFT combines individual and family sessions to get a well-rounded portrait of the patient.

TYPES OF ADOLESCENT THERAPY

Much like adult therapies, adolescent treatment programs are broken down into inpatient and outpatient services. Even seemingly harmless "experimentation" can be cause for alarm with teens, since teens escalate from experimentation to dependence more rapidly than adults. They're also at greater risk of long-term problems from use. For this reason, medical professionals are urged to "screen" teens for signs of substance misuse and direct them to the proper help using programs like SBIRT. Another screening tool used to help determine if an adolescent needs help with substance use is known as CRAFFT. That acronym stands for the first letters of key words in the six questions asked during the screening:

1. Have you ever ridden in a *car* driven by someone (including yourself) who had been using alcohol or drugs?
2. Do you ever use alcohol or drugs to *relax*, feel better about yourself, or fit in?
3. Do you ever use alcohol/drugs when you are by yourself, *alone*?
4. Do you ever *forget* things you did while using alcohol or drugs?
5. Do your family or *friends* ever tell you that you should cut down on your drinking or drug use?
6. Have you gotten into *trouble* while you were using alcohol or drugs?

Doctors perform a CRAFFT assessment to learn out about a patient's relationship with drugs and alcohol.

Sometimes doctors will simplify the CRAFFT method by just asking, "How many times in the past year have you used [DRUG]?" Whichever approach they take, the main thing addiction specialists agree on is that teens just need to be *asked* about their substance use habits. Only through frank conversation will the screening process be effective.

The good news is, a great many adolescent cases can be handled in outpatient settings. This is because addictions are not as far advanced as they are in adult cases, where the body has built up a tolerance to the substance and withdrawal symptoms are more severe. Similar outpatient methods are used with adolescent patients, including cognitive behavioral therapy, motivational incentives, group therapy and 12-step programs

BACK TO SCHOOL

Students transitioning out of intensive therapy back into school are sometimes placed in recovery high schools. These schools may be part of a larger community, though the students are kept together to support one another, avoid social distractions that may cause them to relapse, and focus on new skills learned in therapy. These schools are found all over the country; the Association of Recovery Schools (https://www.recoveryschools.org/) has information about how these schools work and where they are located.

Some kids really benefit from attending a recovery school, where their peers all understand the struggles they go through with sobriety.

specifically designed for teens. Younger patients may be paired up with older members of Alcoholics Anonymous (AA) or Narcotics Anonymous (NA), who serve as their sponsors. Partial hospitalization and inpatient services exist for those teens who have more intense addictions, or whose mental health or family situations require that they be under constant care.

A key component of recovery is creating a balanced life. This means prioritizing the activities that you value most. It also means being honest with yourself and admitting there are areas you need to improve. Those in recovery are urged to think about how they truly want to spend their time, whether they are too focused on one thing—like popularity or a physical appearance—and ways they can take care of both themselves and the others in their lives.

TEXT-DEPENDENT QUESTIONS

1. What are some ways that addiction patterns differ between adolescents and adults?
2. Why is it important to involve family members in an adolescent's recovery?
3. How are therapeutic approaches to use disorder similar in adults and adolescents? How are they different?

RESEARCH PROJECT

Find out what kinds of programs your school and community offer teenagers with abuse issues. For example, interview a guidance counselor or teacher about a recovery high school in your area; ask questions about its history, curriculum, and how it works. Alternately, if there is a peer mentoring program at your school, interview participants to find out what they've learned either as mentors or mentees (people who work with mentors). Write a brief report summarizing your findings. Better yet—if you feel inspired, join up with one of these groups to keep the dialogue going.

FURTHER READING

BOOKS AND ARTICLES

Brody, Jane E. "Effective Addiction Treatment." *New York Times*, February 4, 2013. http://well.blogs.nytimes.com/2013/02/04/effective-addiction-treatment.

Brody, Jane E. "Picking Addiction Help." *New York Times*, February 11, 2013. http://well.blogs.nytimes.com/2013/02/11/picking-addiction-help/.

Jay, Jeff, and Debra Jay. *Love First: A Family's Guide to Intervention*. Center City, MN: Hazelden, 2008.

L., Kathy. *The Intervention Book: Stories and Solutions from Addicts, Professionals, and Families*. San Francisco, CA: Conari Press, 2011.

Steiker, Lori Holleran. *Youth and Substance Abuse: Prevention, Intervention, and Recovery*. Chicago: Lyceum Books, 2016.

ONLINE

The Addiction Recovery Guide. http://www.addictionrecoveryguide.org.

The Fix: Addiction and Recovery, Straight Up. https://www.thefix.com/.

Mayo Clinic. Drug Addiction. http://www.mayoclinic.org/diseases-conditions/drug-addiction/basics/definition/con-20020970

Substance Abuse and Mental Health Services Administration (SAMHSA). http://www.samhsa.gov/.

EDUCATIONAL VIDEOS

Access these videos with your smart phone or use the URLs below to find them online.

 "Why Are Drugs So Hard to Quit?," National Institute on Drug Abuse. "This video explains addiction in simple terms and offers a hotline to help you or a loved one find treatment." https://youtu.be/zV6zKmt7S5E

 "Anyone Can Become Addicted to Drugs," National Institute on Drug Abuse. "You might think that only some types of people can get addicted to drugs. The truth is, it can happen to anyone, whether you're young or old, rich or poor, male or female." https://youtu.be/SY2luGTX7Dk

 "Thoughts on Recovery," National Institute on Drug Abuse. "The most important things I've learned through addiction and recovery." https://youtu.be/nDqojPjkGJI

 "Recovery: What's Research Got to do with It, Part I," National Institute on Drug Abuse. "NIDA TV presents Faces and Voices of Recovery's Executive Director, Pat Taylor, who is interviewed by NIDA's Office of Science Policy and Communications Director, Dr. Jack Stein." https://youtu.be/2M4rYZU48EM

 "Recovery: What's Research Got to do with It, Part II," National Institute on Drug Abuse. "NIDA TV presents Faces and Voices of Recovery's Program Director, Tom Hill, who is interviewed by NIDA's Office of Science Policy and Communications Director, Dr. Jack Stein." https://youtu.be/QYxi4HhpXhw

SERIES GLOSSARY

abstention: actively choosing to not do something.

acute: something that is intense but lasts a short time.

alienation: a sense of isolation or detachment from a larger group.

alleviate: to lessen or relieve.

binge: doing something to excess.

carcinogenic: something that causes cancer.

chronic: ongoing or recurring.

cognitive: having to do with thought.

compulsion: a desire that is very hard or even impossible to resist.

controlled substance: a drug that is regulated by the government.

coping mechanism: a behavior a person learns or develops in order to manage stress.

craving: a very strong desire for something.

decriminalized: something that is not technically legal but is no longer subject to prosecution.

depressant: a substance that slows particular bodily functions.

detoxify: to remove toxic substances (such as drugs or alcohol) from the body.

ecosystem: a community of living things interacting with their environment.

environment: one's physical, cultural, and social surroundings.

genes: units of inheritance that are passed from parent to child and contain information about specific traits and characteristics.

hallucinate: seeing things that aren't there.

hyperconscious: to be intensely aware of something.

illicit: illegal; forbidden by law or cultural custom.

inhibit: to limit or hold back.

interfamilial: between and among members of a family.

metabolize: the ability of a living organism to chemically change compounds.

neurotransmitter: a chemical substance in the brain.

paraphernalia: the equipment used for producing or ingesting drugs, such as pipes or syringes.

physiological: relating to the way an organism functions.

placebo: a medication that has no physical effect and is used to test whether new drugs actually work.

predisposition: to be more inclined or likely to do something.

prohibition: when something is forbidden by law.

recidivism: a falling back into past behaviors, especially criminal ones.

recreation: something done for fun or enjoyment.

risk factors: behaviors, traits, or influences that make a person vulnerable to something.

sobriety: the state of refraining from alcohol or drugs.

social learning: a way that people learn behaviors by watching other people.

stimulant: a class of drug that speeds up bodily functions.

stressor: any event, thought, experience, or biological or chemical function that causes a person to feel stress.

synthetic: made by people, often to replicate something that occurs in nature.

tolerance: the state of needing more of a particular substance to achieve the same effect.

traffic: to illegally transport people, drugs, or weapons to sell throughout the world.

withdrawal: the physical and psychological effects that occur when a person with a use disorder suddenly stops using substances.

INDEX

ABOUT THE AUTHOR

Michael Centore is a writer and editor. He has helped produce many titles for a variety of publishers, including memoirs, cookbooks, and educational materials, among others. He has authored several previous volumes for Mason Crest, including titles in the Major Nations in a Global World and North American Natural Resources series. His essays have appeared in the *Los Angeles Review of Books, Killing the Buddha, Mockingbird,* and other print- and web-based publications. He lives in Connecticut.

ABOUT THE ADVISOR

Sara Becker, Ph.D. is a clinical researcher and licensed clinical psychologist specializing in the treatment of adolescents with substance use disorders. She is an Assistant Professor (Research) in the Center for Alcohol and Addictions Studies at the Brown School of Public Health and the Evaluation Director of the New England Addiction Technology Transfer Center. Dr. Becker received her Ph.D. in Clinical Psychology from Duke University and completed her clinical residency at Harvard Medical School's McLean Hospital. She joined the Center for Alcohol and Addictions Studies as a postdoctoral fellow and transitioned to the faculty in 2011. Dr. Becker directs a program of research funded by the National Institute on Drug Abuse that explores novel ways to improve the treatment of adolescents with substance use disorders. She has authored over 30 peer-reviewed publications and book chapters and serves on the Editorial Board of the *Journal of Substance Abuse Treatment*.

PHOTO CREDITS